Audition Songs for Female Singers

Broadway Favorites

Page	Title	CD Track
2	As If We Never Said Goodbye	1
8	Cabaret	2
17	Don't Cry for Me Argentina	3
23	I Don't Know How to Love Him	4
28	I Dreamed a Dream	5
32	If My Friends Could See Me Now	6
39	Memory	7
45	My Favorite Things	8
53	What I Did for Love	9
57	The Winner Takes It All	10

ISBN 978-1-4234-8946-7

Music Sales America

EXCLUSIVELY DISTRIBUTED BY

7777 W. BLUEMOUND RD. P.O. BOX 13819 MILWAUKEE, WI 53213

For all works contained herein:
Unauthorized copying, arranging, adapting, recording, Internet posting, public performance,
or other distribution of the printed or recorded music in this publication is an infringement of copyright.
Infringers are liable under the law.

Visit Hal Leonard Online at
www.halleonard.com

AS IF WE NEVER SAID GOODBYE

from SUNSET BOULEVARD

Music by ANDREW LLOYD WEBBER
Lyrics by DON BLACK and CHRISTOPHER HAMPTON,
with contributions by AMY POWERS

© Copyright 1993 Andrew Lloyd Webber licensed to The Really Useful Group Ltd.
International Copyright Secured   All Rights Reserved

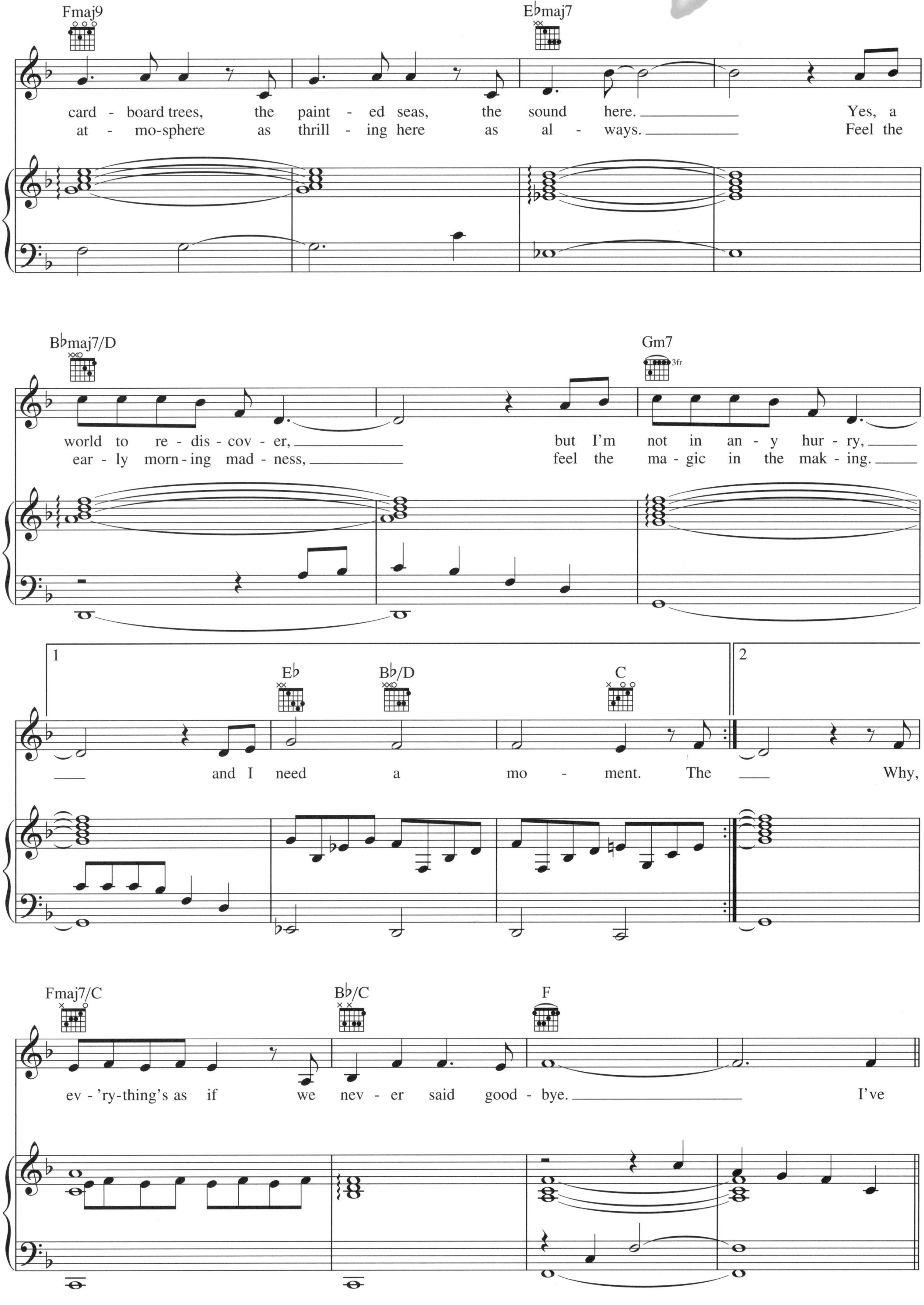

3

Fmaj9 | **E♭maj7**

card - board trees, the paint - ed seas, the sound here. Yes, a
at - mo-sphere as thrill - ing here as al - ways. Feel the

B♭maj7/D | **Gm7**

world to re - dis - cov - er, but I'm not in an - y hur - ry,
ear - ly morn - ing mad - ness, feel the ma - gic in the mak - ing.

1. **E♭** **B♭/D** **C** **2.**

and I need a mo - ment. The Why,

Fmaj7/C | **B♭/C** | **F**

ev - 'ry-thing's as if we nev - er said good - bye. I've

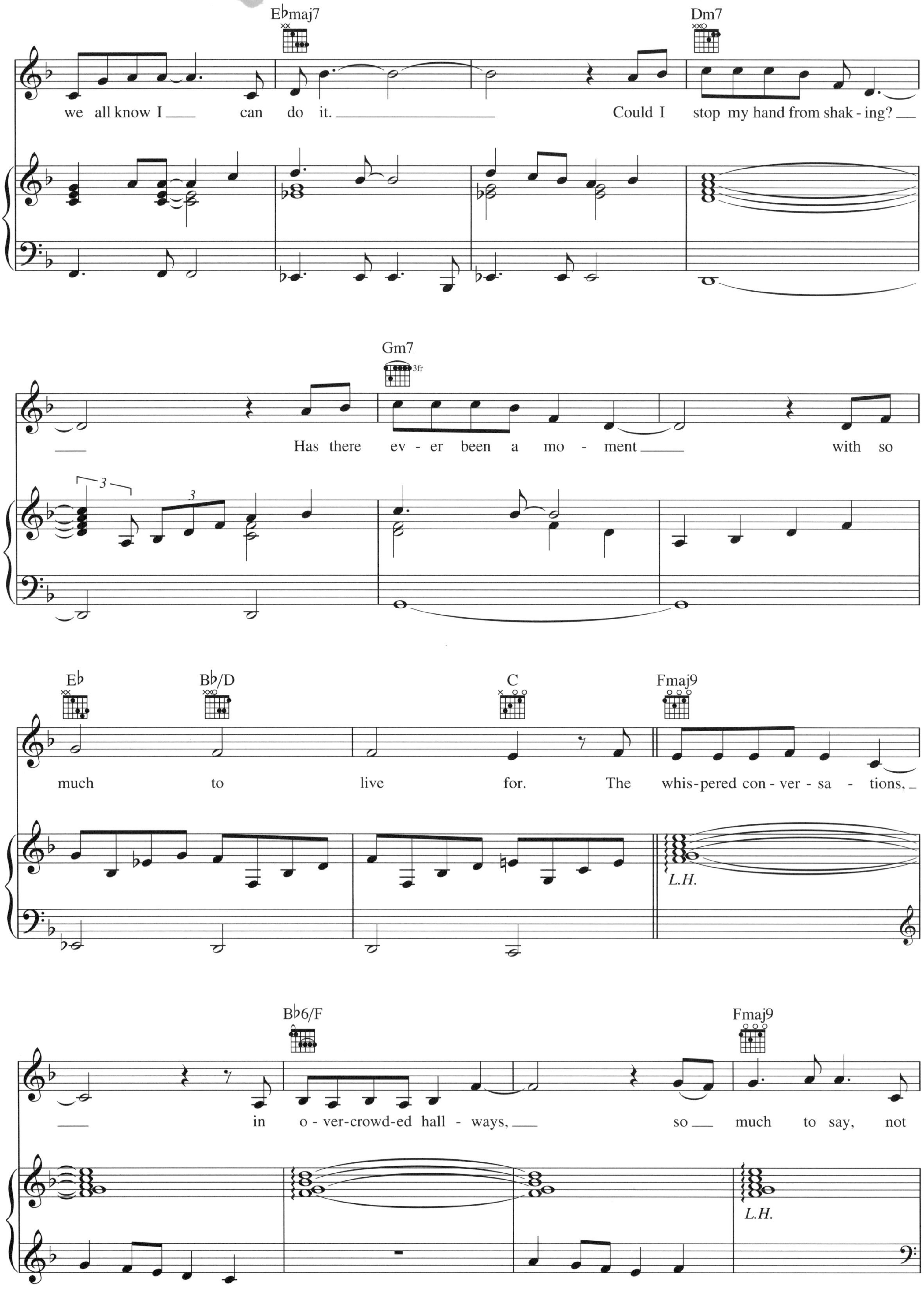
E♭maj7
Dm7
we all know I ___ can do it. ___ Could I stop my hand from shak - ing? ___
Gm7
3fr
___ Has there ev - er been a mo - ment ___ with so
E♭
B♭/D
C
Fmaj9
much to live for. The whis-pered con - ver - sa - tions, ___
L.H.
B♭6/F
Fmaj9
___ in o - ver-crowd-ed hall - ways, ___ so ___ much to say, not
L.H.

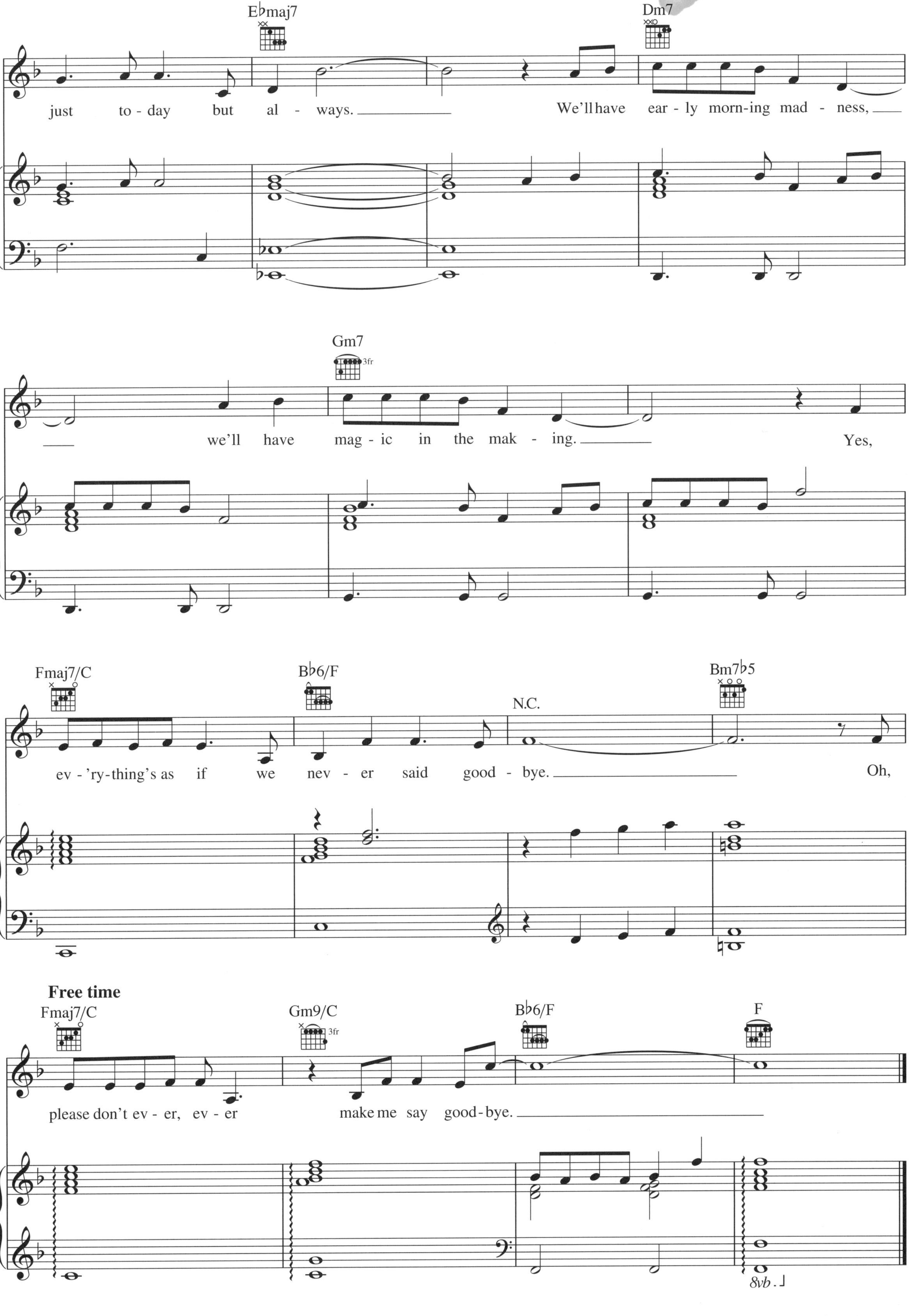
E♭maj7
Dm7
just to - day but al - ways.
We'll have ear - ly morn - ing mad - ness,
Gm7
3fr
we'll have mag - ic in the mak - ing.
Yes,
Fmaj7/C
B♭6/F
N.C.
Bm7♭5
ev - 'ry - thing's as if we nev - er said good - bye.
Oh,
Free time
Fmaj7/C
Gm9/C
3fr
B♭6/F
F
please don't ev - er, ev - er make me say good - bye.
8vb

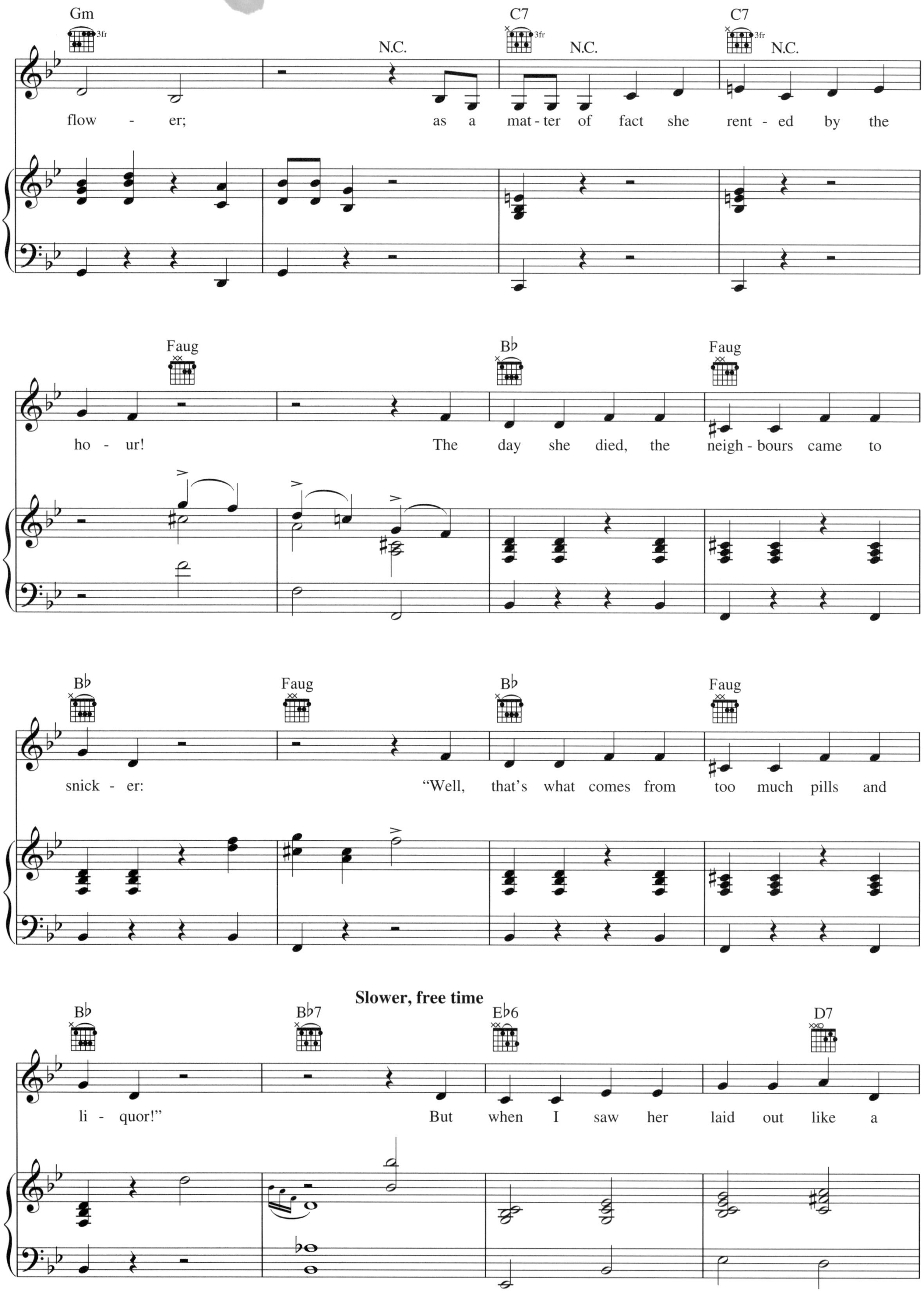
Gm
N.C.
C7
N.C.
C7
N.C.
flow - er; as a mat - ter of fact she rent - ed by the
Faug
B♭
Faug
ho - ur! The day she died, the neigh - bours came to
B♭
Faug
B♭
Faug
snick - er: "Well, that's what comes from too much pills and
Slower, free time
B♭
B♭7
E♭6
D7
li - quor!" But when I saw her laid out like a

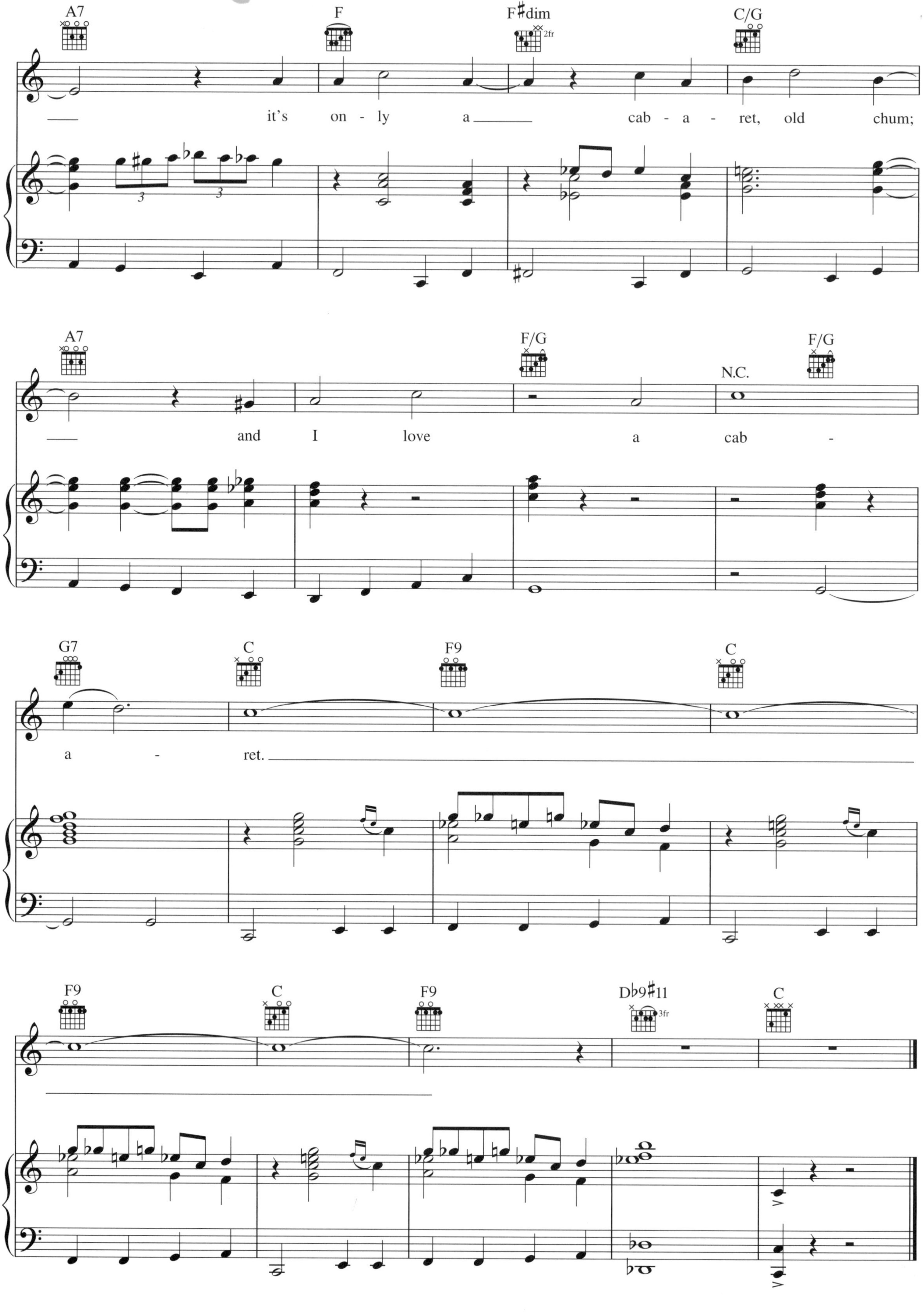
A7
F
F♯dim
C/G
it's on - ly a cab - a - ret, old chum;
A7
F/G
N.C.
F/G
and I love a cab -
G7
C
F9
C
a - ret.
F9
C
F9
D♭9♯11
C

DON'T CRY FOR ME ARGENTINA
from EVITA

Words by TIM RICE
Music by ANDREW LLOYD WEBBER

I DON'T KNOW HOW TO LOVE HIM
from JESUS CHRIST SUPERSTAR

Words by TIM RICE
Music by ANDREW LLOYD WEBBER

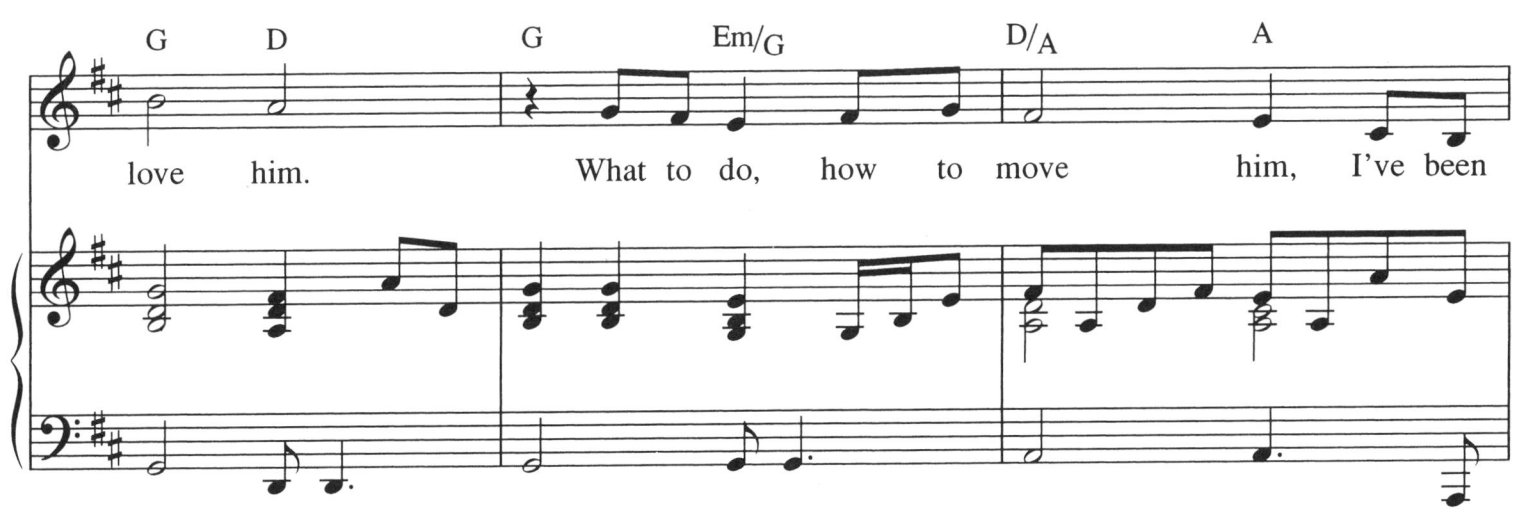

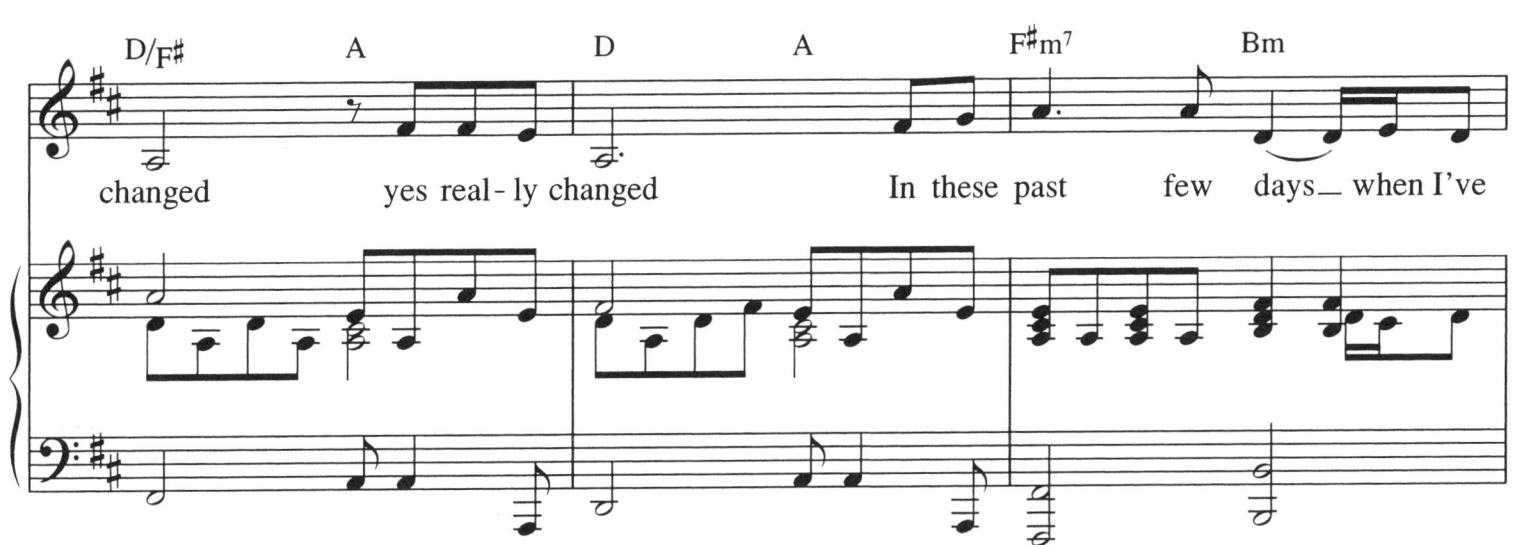

Copyright © 1971 UNIVERSAL / MCA MUSIC LTD.
Copyright Renewed
All Rights for the U.S. and Canada Controlled and Administered by UNIVERSAL MUSIC CORP.
All Rights Reserved   Used by Permission

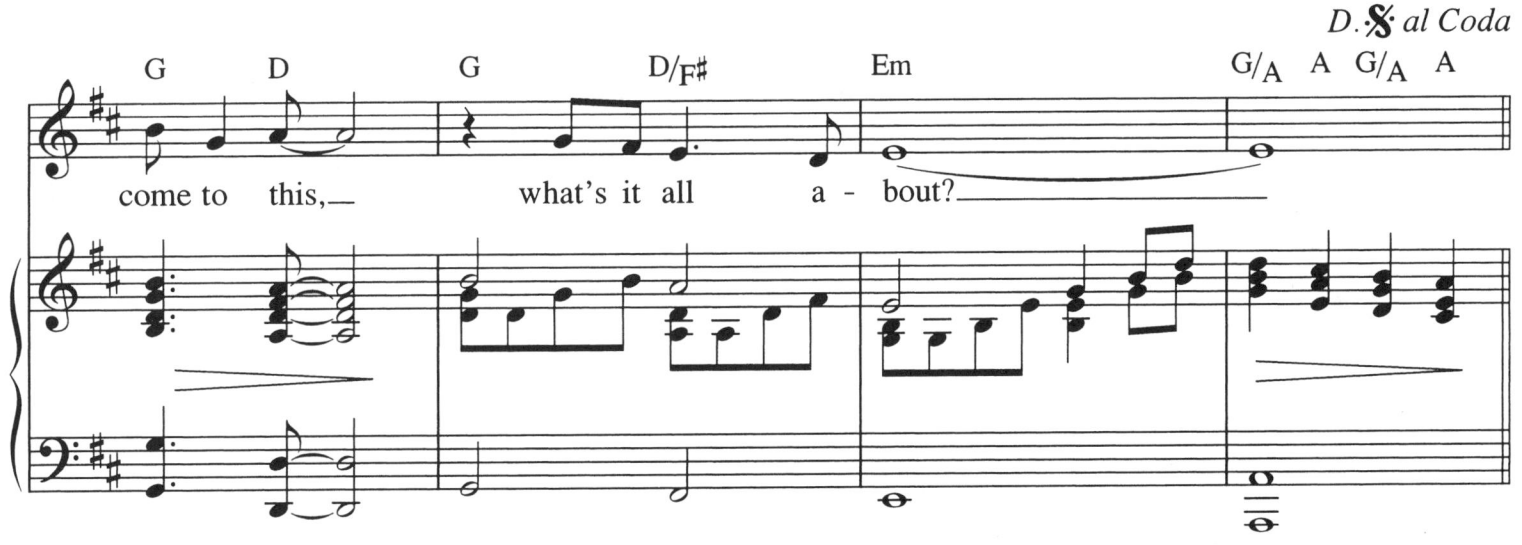

I DREAMED A DREAM
from LES MISERABLES

Music by CLAUDE-MICHEL SCHÖNBERG
Lyrics by ALAIN BOUBLIL, JEAN-MARC NATEL
and HERBERT KRETZMER

Music and Lyrics Copyright © 1980 by Editions Musicales Alain Boublil
English Lyrics Copyright © 1986 by Alain Boublil Music Ltd. (ASCAP)
Mechanical and Publication Rights for the U.S.A. Administered by Alain Boublil Music Ltd. (ASCAP) c/o Joel Faden & Co., Inc.,
MLM 250 West 57th Street, 26th Floor, New York, NY 10107, Tel. (212) 246-7203, Fax (212) 246-7217, mwlock@joelfaden.com
International Copyright Secured.   All Rights Reserved.   This music is copyright.   Photocopying is illegal.
All Performance Rights Restricted.

IF MY FRIENDS COULD SEE ME NOW
from SWEET CHARITY

Music by CY COLEMAN
Lyrics by DOROTHY FIELDS

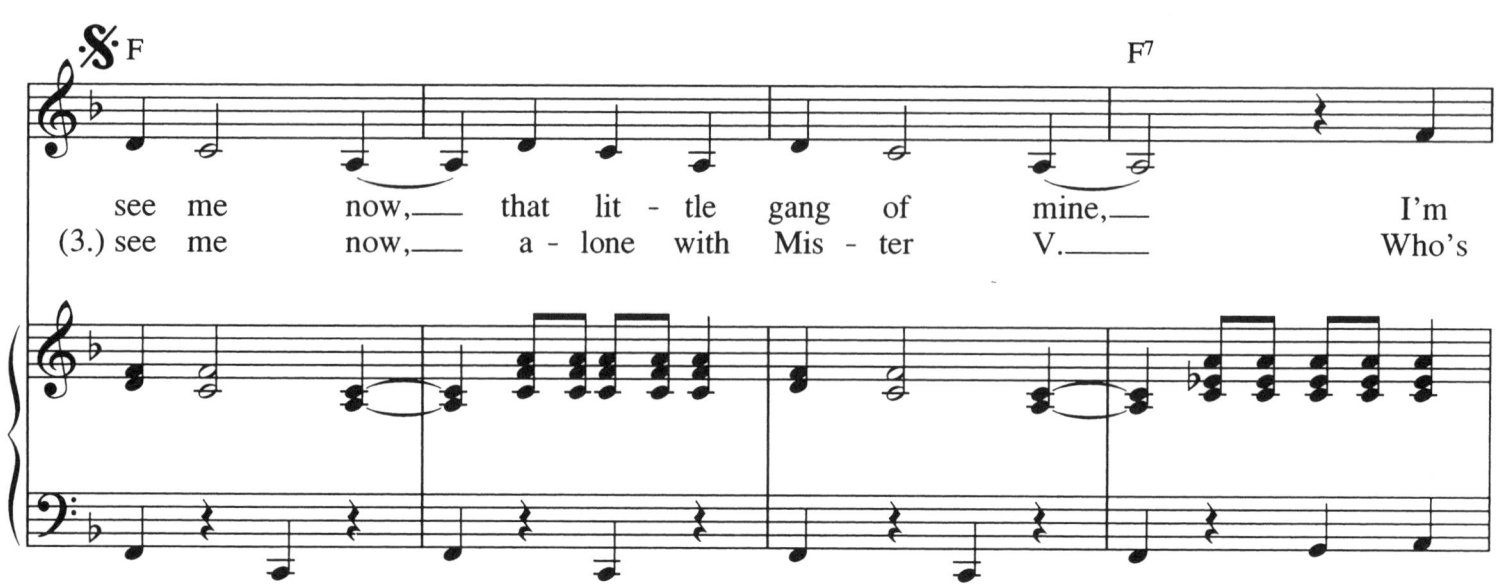

Copyright © 1965 Notable Music Company, Inc. and Lida Enterprises
Copyright Renewed
All Rights Administered by Chrysalis Music
All Rights Reserved   Used by Permission

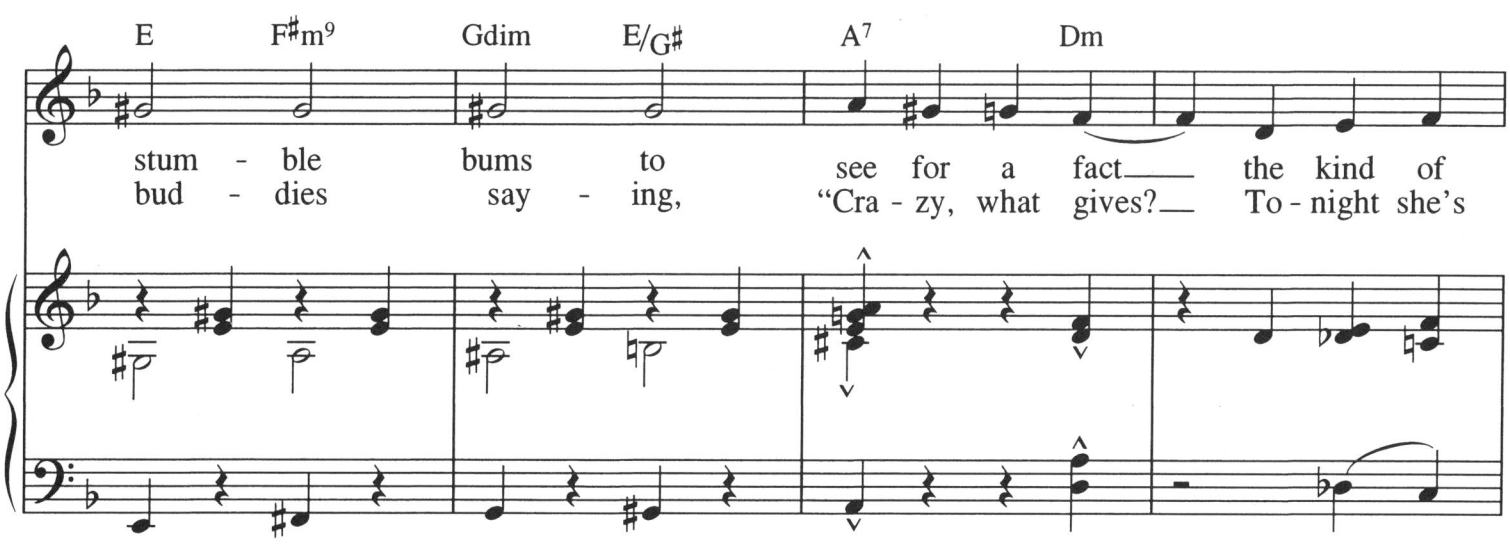
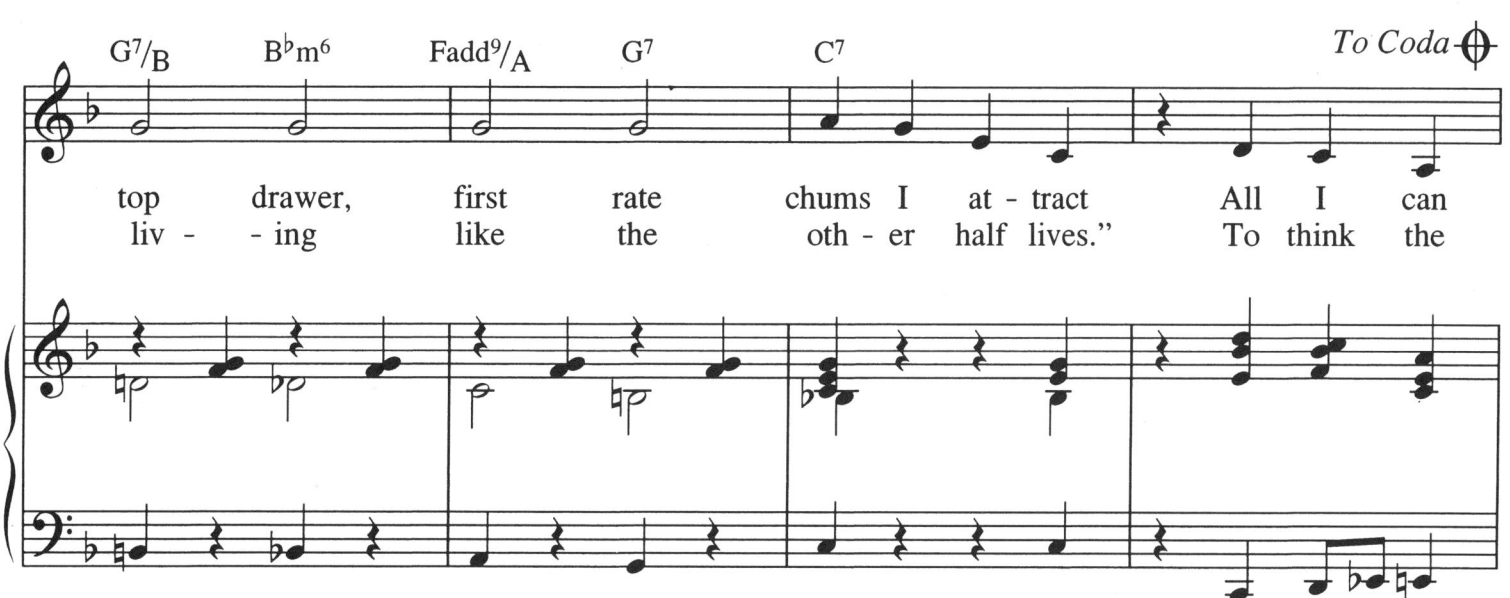

MY FAVORITE THINGS
from THE SOUND OF MUSIC

Lyrics by OSCAR HAMMERSTEIN II
Music by RICHARD RODGERS

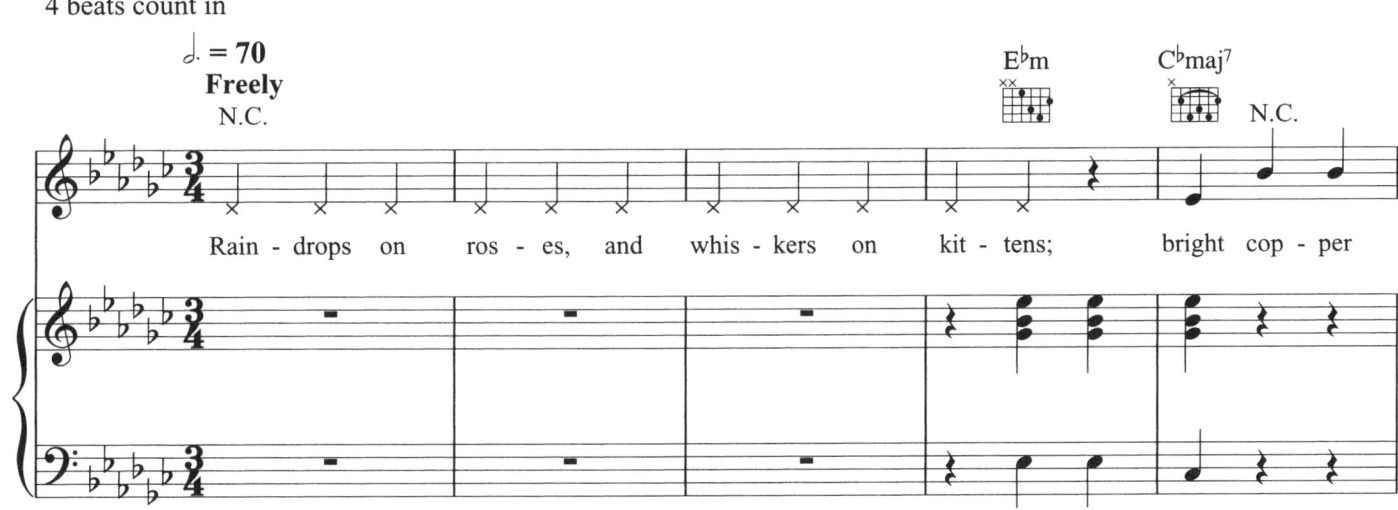

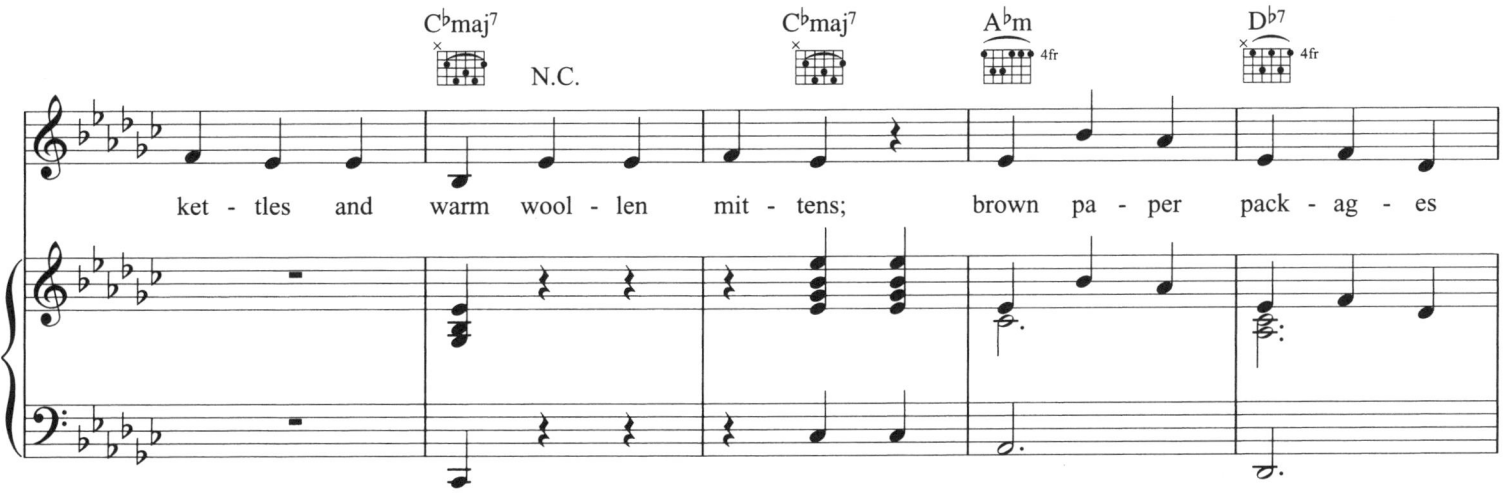

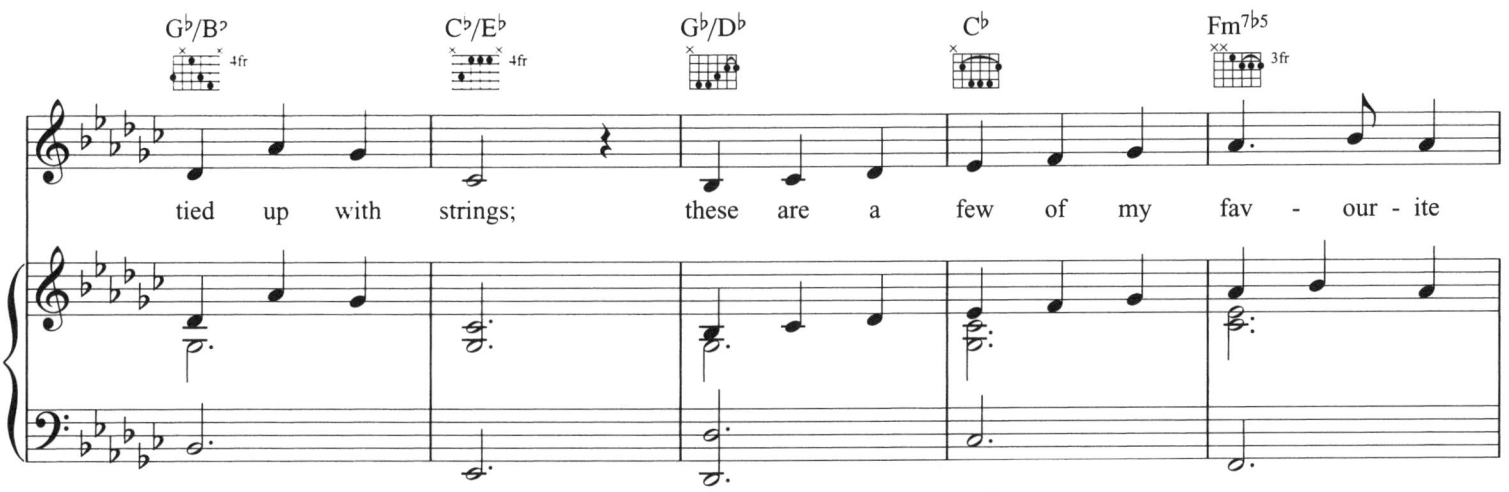

Copyright © 1959 by Richard Rodgers and Oscar Hammerstein II
Copyright Renewed
WILLIAMSON MUSIC owner of publication and allied rights throughout the world
International Copyright Secured   All Rights Reserved

WHAT I DID FOR LOVE
from A CHORUS LINE

Music by MARVIN HAMLISCH
Lyric by EDWARD KLEBAN

Verse 3:
But tell me, does she kiss like I used to kiss you,
Does it feel the same when she calls your name?
Somewhere deep inside,
You must know I miss you,
But what can I say,
Rules must be obeyed.
The judges will decide the likes of me abide,
Spectators of the show always staying low.

Verse 4:
I don't wanna talk
If it makes you feel sad
And I understand you've come to shake my hand.
I apologise if it makes you feel bad
Seeing me so tense,
No self-confidence.
The winner takes it all.
The winner takes it all.

CD TRACK LISTING

CD TRACK	TITLE	MUSIC PAGE
1	**As If We Never Said Goodbye**	2
2	**Cabaret**	8
3	**Don't Cry for Me Argentina**	17
4	**I Don't Know How to Love Him**	23
5	**I Dreamed a Dream**	28
6	**If My Friends Could See Me Now**	32
7	**Memory**	39
8	**My Favorite Things**	45
9	**What I Did for Love**	53
10	**The Winner Takes It All**	57